Extranjera

Extranjera

Lola Haskins
Lola Haskins

Story Line Press
1998

First American Printing

Published by Story Line Press, Inc.,
Three Oaks Farm, Brownsville, OR 97327

This publication was made possible thanks in part to the generous support of the Nicholas Roerich Museum, the Andrew W. Mellon Foundation, the Charles Schwab Corporation Foundation and our individual contributors.

Book design by Chiquita Babb

Cover photograph: American *Vogue* Cover, November 1, 1945, by Erwin Blumenfeld. *Courtesy Victoria and Albert Museum.*

Library of Congress Cataloging-in-Publication Data

Haskins, Lola.
Extranjera / Lola Haskins.
p. cm.
ISBN 1-885266-57-X
1. Americans—Travel—Mexico—Poetry. 2. Mexico—Poetry.
I. Title.
PS3558A7238E98 1998
811'.54—DC21 97-48901
CIP

Acknowledgments

I would like to thank Margaret McKinnon, Sarah Carey, and Andrea Hollander Budy for support beyond what I can return.

Some of the poems in this book were published in the following periodicals:

Americas Review: Her Story, Lo Que Yo Me Enteré, Donde Está La Estrella

Artful Dodge: El Gran Eclipse de México, Wait for Us, Final

Boulevard: Waiting for the Bus

Caprice: In the Market, Jesus; La Senora de Garcìa Marcos Considers

Crazyhorse: El Mercado

Free Lunch: The Meaning of Taquitos

International Quarterly: Los Viejitos

Kestrel: Nopales, The Man in the Large and Glittering Hat

Kalliope: Angel del Temblor

London Magazine: Ligia, El Milagro

London Review of Books: Blood, Casa, Ligia

Missouri Review: Juan of the Angels, Cuando Morimos, El Dia de Los Muertos, The Carver of Masks, El Café, Lengthening Light, Three Views from the Latin American Summit

Ploughshares: Uchepas

Tampa Review: Salvation in a Catholic Country, Dog

Table of Contents

México 1

1

Eclipse 5
Wait for Us 000
The Pyramids at Tsuntsintsan 7
Monday Morning in the Plaza de Armas 8
Street Level 9
Three Views from the Latin American Summit 10
Roofs 12
Salvation in a Catholic Country 13
Los Viejitos 14

2

Sobre Transportes del Norte 17
Catedral 18
Nopales 19
El Milagro 20
Her Story 21
The Fish They Call Sierra 22
La Estrella 24
Caballos 25
Peluquero 26
Cuando Morimos 27
Nombres 28

Lengthening Light 31

3

The Man in the Large and Glittering Hat 35
El Café 36
Ja Ja 37
El Mercado 38
The Carver of Masks 39
The Platanillos 40
Ligia 42
Straw 43
Angel del Temblor 44
Juan of the Angels 46
Waiting for the Bus 48
The Liberator 50
La Senora de Garcia-Marcos Considers 51

4

Uchepas 55
Guayabas 56
The Meaning of Taquitos 57
In the Market Jesús Cleans Fish 58
Dog 59
Casa 60
Blood 61
El Grito de Dolores 62
Chiles: A Birthday Poem 63

Final 65

México

I have lived here before but always
I have retreated. It is afraid
staying in a language where you
were not born. Where vowels seem
soft but throb mercilessly on
like this bruja sun which will
not die, but burns into the night.

I have looked in this mirror
and looked down. I have sung
canciones to make me weep,
and denied the tears. I have
never owned those receptacles
which hold hearts. It is afraid.

I have said no to the flies in me.
I have refused to tongue the red
and juicy seeds heaped in cups.
But this time, though I climb faintly
up the bus's purring stairs,
though at first it is afraid to see,
this time I say Yes. Yes I am
willing now. Yes foreign is a word
for fear. Yes I am coming home.

1

Eclipse

The government says that women
will not birth monsters,
that pigs will still nurse their young,
that corn will not shrink to ash.
But who believes the government?

It is noon and night is falling.
You and I look only down.
We are afraid of what may be
glowing in the air.
We know that there are

some truths so terrible
that to face them
would whiten our eyes forever.

Wait for Us

Watchful boys, gleams in their pockets,
circle the Plaza where a television
explains *El Gran Eclipse de México*,
as though the moon crossing the sun
belongs to this nation whose anthem
shouts of war.
                    This is Uruápan.
You can walk under the palms in
the Parque Nacional, where banyans
cast complicated roots, and bananas
hang in thick fingers. You can hear
the shouts of children practicing
insults and fighting- the many uses
of teeth.
                    But now it is night
and the foreigner is at risk.
The soft white foreigner. We walk
fast. They begin to follow us.
They quicken. *Espéranos*, they call.

The Pyramids at Tsuntsintsan

Tried to rise, like an old man
from a deep chair, but collapsed
into themselves, not all at once
but by the weather slowly,
the way our son, who will soon
leave home, stays out more and
more.
          Tiny signs, half-gone in
green, brought us here. We
climbed angry, through the rank
smells of flowers and snake.
We struggled for footing on
the scattered hill. We argued.
Til the pyramids struck us dumb.

Monday Morning in the Plaza de las Armas

The tiny plastic soldiers dangle
from their parachutes. They litter
the power lines and the higher
branches of trees. Red and blue and
yellow shreds punctuate the scene.
The air is grey. It is very still.

Not like yesterday when the Plaza
teemed with *Papi! Mami! Por Favor!*
and vendors handed over the little
men, and balloons, and dulces spiny
with coconut. Then BANG and BANG
as small fists clutched what were
not any more balloons, and soldiers
which Paco or Ana or Luis had thought
to take home and keep forever sailed
out of reach and no Papi, however
rich, could buy them back again.

The soldiers rock a little as a wind
comes up, rock softly, like lullabies.

Street Level

He brandishes a fan of fly swatters,
yellow and blue and green.
Para las moscas, he sings.
And *Barrato Barrato*, like the buzzing
of flies. He is perhaps five.
Later he will build castles with his sister
from tar that has been heaped in the street.
His dark brown hands will turn black.
The light will fail. Molding the tar in
battlements, he will be completely happy.

Three Views from the Latin American Summit

Guadalajara, Jalisco 1991

i

Important men hold forth to an ocean
of campesinos with armbands and banners.
Slogans fly like spray. On the edges
of the crowd shoeshine boys quote
prices. After, they say they meant
per shoe. And foreigners pay,
their faces red for their poor Spanish.

ii

She leans slack to the wall.
Bright flies cluster where
her eyes ooze. A visitor in
a grey suit, his belly ripe as
a fat papaya, breaks his stride.
She palms the coins.
Her hand is empty. Her hand
has always been empty.

iii

In the Plaza del Catedrál they have
sandblasted the nudes which shine
fresh green, their instruments
in their arms. The unswept sand
crunches underfoot. At any moment
a wave may break, here over this city,
hundreds of miles from the coast.

Roofs

Of banged-on tin that never shone.
Twisted scrap-tin full of holes so
light dots the dirt floor inside.

Of red tiles cured in sun, lapping
over like a dance, the way a husband
curves into his wife's cupped body.

Of banana leaves, wing on wing.
A child lies inside, wasted by
the sick water. His eyes are flame.

Salvation in a Catholic Country

As we enter Gabriel palms
our key. He slides it
across the slick desk.
He knows our number.
He knows where we will go
from here, the elevators
by which we will rise.
He knows the doors
that will open by themselves.

In La Concordia, life
is simple: the smell of
arepas, ascending the air
shaft, the chitter of maids
watching the soaps in
the next room, the heavy
cleansing rains that stop
before we can even count
our sins. This is thin air.
Climbing these hills,
how easily we leave
breath behind.

Los Viejitos

They leer from market stalls,
lean crudely carved in their
hundreds, on sticks of canes.
In the better hotels you can
see them dance. First though,
their conjunto sqeaks a set,
its violin so out of tune a dog
would run. And then at last
the old men, bent double,
enter in a twist. They pause.
They stomp their canes.
They exhibit, one by one.
Finally, in a burst of claps
they clog off-stage. When
they lift their masks we glimpse
that even these are children.
They will overwhelm us all.

2

Sobre Transportes del Norte

He leans across the aisle, and points
out my window to a field where three
streams of water gush straight up.
Agua caliente, he says. *De la tierra*.
We are nearing Zamora. The bus
slides by the blue wall of the plastics
factory. PRD, says the wall. And,
PRI. All Mexico is coming to a boil.

Yo soy de Salinas, he says. *California*.
He pulls his wallet out of his jeans,
scratches his undershirted stomach,
and passes me three folded sheets.
See? he says. Tickets. They are damp
from riding under him. *Drunk driving*
he says proudly. *One more, and they*
put me in jail. I like cerveza too much.
And he grins, and his teeth are so white
I think they would glow in the dark.

He folds the papers, leans back, puts
them away again. We are passing
fields of maguey, full of broken glass
which glitters in the sun. I am foreign.
There is so much I do not understand.

Catedral

Below the gold Virgin, notes fade.
My son in California would die
but I prayed to you. Bless you
that Tía Angela is safe.
Besides
the notes, four wordless snapshots
from a photo booth. Young boys.
Under each is taped a car key.
Protect them Holy Mother, where
they go.
On her knees an old woman
is crossing the stone. Her rebozo
trails its fringe of black and blue.
When she reaches the altar rail,
she opens her palms.
She feels them fill with light.

Nopales

They start before dawn, baskets airy on their backs,
two old sisters, climbing the rock-strewn hill.
In the forest of cacti they turn small, reaching
up to slice the thick leaves from their stems.
Already Rosa's thumb is festering. She scrapes
at it with her knife. The sharp spines break,
burrow deeper. She wonders where her children
sleep, gone these years across the border.
Wading at night. Running from her to L. A.,
as far away as the stars.
                                        When Teresita starts
for home, Rosa follows. They heft the baskets
from their backs. The chickens squawk and scatter.
Teresita squats, fans the coals to flame.
                                                                Rosa
feels a flush, like that of a young girl, spread
across her face. *La Virgen*. Walking towards
them in her blue rebozo. The light beginning
over the hills is the light of miracles.

El Milagro

Adela sees the pig ascend to Heaven.
One moment he's rooting in the muddy
street. The next he's in a golden
cloud rising above the red-tile roofs.
He swirls and vanishes. *Alleluia*
Adela hears from the catedral and all
the bells start ringing. Surely this
was some holy pig to be taken to live
among God and all His angels. Perhaps
he was never a pig at all. Adela
makes the sign of the cross. As her
shaking fingers calm, Adela knows
she will never again eat pork.

Her Story

Her palms pale with masa.
The tortillas on her drum are freckled moons.
Black braids lie down her back. Her apron

is fading the way dusk
blurs the edges of the island so its shrine
turns to air. When the bus plunged off

the twisting road,
like a bird folded sharp, and her brother's flesh
charred to meat, she did not care about God

nor the flaming wreck
that called itself Three Stars of Gold.
She lives alone now, speaks to no one but

the fish in the lake,
that rise to the scraps she throws, then
vanish into the twilit water like prayer.

The Fish They Call Sierra

i

They name it for how it leaps, for its wish to
become sky.

They name it for the high air between the peaks of
its tail.

They name it for what they crave- mountains thick
as fish, swimming in their thousands towards
the horizon forever.

ii

The cheeks of Tarascan men are smooth
as the sheened red clay their women
shape to birds, from whose mouths
water pours.
Mornings the men launch
their boats. They cast nets into the fog.
When the nets begin to move in
their hands, they lean into what they
cannot see, and pull, until the fog itself
turns silver.
And they go on pulling until
they are up to their knees in fish, until
there is no place on the bottom of the boat,
which does not move.

iii

Rosalia slits the last sierra
and removes its curled insides.
She dips her knife in the lake.
The pulse at her wrist turns
cool. The soft blood drifts
away. On her hip the baby stirs,
unclenches the star of his hand.

La Estrella

The star is everywhere, says Miguel.
Today I saw it on a wall.

It is on the forehead of the Virgen,
says Mamá, and *it is outside too*,

in the dark, higher than the arches
of the catedral. And also here,

says Miguel, opening his fist.
This one fell down one day.

I caught it on its way to the sea.
And mira, Mamá, all those. And

they lean their heads out the window
where there is no glass,

out into the night, where mariachis
of stars are glittering,

hard and bright as jewels on a shoe.
Miguel looks down at his bare toes.

His mother picks him up. His hand
is closed, holding his star safe.

Caballos

The painted caballos of the carneval
have been covered for the night. Under
that black cloth they gallop still,
hard around the mirrored dark, circling
the small gold lights to the organ's
wheezy tune, and always on their backs
the warm hands of niños, their chubby legs
gripping as though the caballos were going
somewhere wild, beyond the earshot
of criadas, gossiping in the back patio,
to places their parents can never know
who think the children safe in bed
when they've kissed their drowsy
cheeks goodnight, and shut the door.

Peluquero

On the street a man is losing his hair.
He slumps, head bent, neck exposed.
Across the man's shoulders, stuck to
a grubby towel, blue-black clippings
strew, and around the man's huaraches,
wetly on his bare toes, the thick hairs
rain.

So easily could he die, and by
this graffittied wall and on such a day
as this, in spring, having sat down
harmless, thinking nothing

as around
the corner a sudden camión comes
blasting, and the peluquero leaps
away, lurches into the man's chair,
bright scissors in his forward hand.

Cuando Morimos

Hernán fell. He used not to be afraid
climbing scaffolds, his hammer bouncing at
his hip the way a woodpecker bangs a tree,
used never to fear walking that high slant,
his mouth studded with nails.

Now we carry his box through the streets,
the box in which he lies, his hat in his hands.
It is a long way out of town, and dust coats us
all. We have put on masks: birds and jaguars,
the faces of moths. Hernán's is the only true
face. And Hernán fell.

The building rises which Hernán built.
El Palacio del Gobierno it will be, where
el senor presidente municipal will sit, the
new palacio whose roof is strong, whose
air is full of falling. And we will all of us
do business in its rooms.

Nombres

We name our streets for desire. *Calzada de la Independencia* rotates through the destinations of buses which bulge like heavy bellies, which pass the rooftops lined with police, bristling with assault rifles. There is an election. Anger will lose again. *PRI* says God and the ballots of the dead.

We name our children for God. Jesus for the glowing heart and blessing hand. Jesus for the peace we crave, carrying warm tortillas home. Maria for the Virgin. And we wear tight skirts and blouses which curve to make a man's hand itch as we dream in streets lined with brides, white as first communions. Then we pass through those windows and on the other side...How dark it is. How we cannot breathe.

We name our holidays for the dead. We eat buñuelos iced with skulls and we play with tiny skeletons, jointed and dancing. We feast for our dead mothers and uncles. We breathe the fragrant steam and let the tamales alone. We drink cerveza into the candled night and celebrate that life is short.

Lengthening Light

Y ser como ese sol que lento expira
Algo muy luminoso que se pierde...
Miguel Nájera

My shadow over the plaza is growing long.
The stalls of bracelets are gleaming,
lapus lazuli, lazy light like half-shut eyes.
My skin in the late day is darkening.

The shade is slow leaves slowly joining.
Soon it will be lost for the sun will leave it
like a faithless lover over and over
gets up and goes away until all shade is

one shadow over the plaza and why have I
come? It is afraid, staying in a language
where I was not born. Yet I am learning
words for a voice known in any tongue

as the certainty of night arrives and I
await the stars with such fear I cannot
tell you. Have you noticed old women,
their arms circled in lapis, a ring

on every wrinkled finger? I take a table,
ask for cafe con leche. I sip it,
slowly, making it last. I am admiring
the beautiful lengthening light.

3

The Man in the Large and Glittering Hat

Thinks the stars flurried down
and settled on his head.

He walks between the rickety
tables   his guitar poised

looking into the women's eyes.
Hesitation is enough. He is

singing of kisses. Natalia imagines
him lifting her hair, to reveal

the place no larger than a centavo,
just behind her ear. She imagines

the damp of his lips. He's a bobo,
she thinks. In her dream his hands

are all over her. She looks up, sees
the hat, like a galaxy, on its peg.

El Café

Stone arches frame the table where a man has joined Melinda. She does not know him. They order coffee. He sets his briefcase down, rests one hand on the table. The hand is a furred spider, the kind that lives under wood. Once there was a hurricane off the coast, such blowing rain, such wind, that the avocados that lined the hills were blasted from their roots. After, she went with Papá to see. He rolled a downed branch, like a body, with his foot, and from it there crawled such a spider.

The coffee comes, in tiny cups. She adds sugar. He taps a long ash from his cigarette. Melinda, who has never smoked, is seized with the desire to begin. The man pulls charts from his briefcase, lays them on the table. "Here", he says, and "There", touching the numbers as if they were cities. Melinda says "Yes", and "Oh, I see", and her breath is growing short. She licks the foam from the creamy edge of her cup.

A boy, bent under a load of straw masks, pauses at their table. He shakes one out. Melinda buys it, puts it on. She leaves with the man. In his room there is an altar, a Virgin surrounded by flowers. He makes love to Melinda's woven face. Later, she goes home. Her husband asks her about the coffee in that cafe. Is it still black and strong, a bullet in the throat? Did she enjoy lingering? Melinda shows him the mask.

Ja Ja

The guard at the jewelry store sights along the barrel of his rifle. He follows the pretty girl, keeping her chest in the center of his cross-hairs. She sees him from the corner of her eye. She hurries. The tiny heart on her ankle-chain jingles busily. She turns the corner. He lowers the gun. *Ja Ja.*

El Mercado

In the center of the mercado
the dark and crowded aisles open to the sky.
Here Alicia stands one early morning,
when all the stalls are covered and tied
as if by families moving far away. And
she rubs the bruises with her thumb
deliberately, in one direction, as
one would rub silver to raise
a shine.
And Alicia thinks this dawn is
home, not Miguel with the black crescents
under his nails and the creases in his
knuckles black. Who pressed hard against
her, flattening her breasts. Not Miguel
with his mouth full of rage, ready
to spit it on her and, when she moved
back, ready to show her what he
could do.
The first rays of sun streak
the plaza. Everywhere, the covers
are coming off. There are shoes and
belts and saddles for sale. There is
rope. No one was leaving after all.

The Carver of Masks

He works the knife.
Thin shavings fall curled,
with the faint scent of burns.
He is making slits.
Through such slits one can hardly see. One is
forever eight,
peering through cracks at Mamá's
screams
until his mouth is stopped
by Papá's borracho
hand.
The mouth's a gash, a slash of blood surprise.
He works faster,
cuts the suggestion of a nose, two
holes, like a snout.
Pig, he thinks, and wipes his
knife on his jeans.

The Platanillos

Mira, the child says, pointing.
The platanillos are bleeding.

You are only little, says her mother,
looking up from the river

where she is washing small underpants
against the rocks. *Bring me that soap.*

The child fetches the thick bar. She
looks up. The sky is darkening.

Jaime went to live with God. Red
leaked from his eyes and ears.

Jaime was even smaller than she is.
They light candles for him every mass

but sometimes the candles go out.
Maybe Jaime is angry. The sky

turns black. There is the smell
of burnt wick. It begins to rain.

Mamá! calls the child. *Mamá!*
Her mother goes on with her work.

The child scrambles up the bank. When
she brushes against the platanillos,

blood comes off on her hands.

Ligia

The family sleeps. Their hammocks
sway gently, like boats on air.
The casa fills with their slow
breathing.
                There is a black swan,
painted on a plate. Ligia pumps
water over her. The swan shakes
glaze from her feet.
                                Ligia leans
dreaming, elbows propped on the
splintered windowsill. The swan
has settled on the dim lake,
just out from shore. She floats
there, so beautiful. The moon
silvers the mesh of Antonio's nets,
between the house and the swan,
where he has spread them to dry.

Straw

A man's sombrero with its one
tiny tassel

A woman's broom,
to gather what has fallen
and return it to the air

Swans and tied stars
hung in strings

What the child rocking in his
hammock dreams:

That the light he sees is made
of grass

That the most beautiful pájaros
are grass also

and he hears their far calls,
like wheat, whispering
in a field

Angel del Temblor

Fallen bronze head, your welds apart,
your huge and gentle body broken
as Teresa rebozoed in the garden
of the museum, Teresa lurching,
fallen as an angel after the quake,
the last to be made whole.

Teresa likes tequila best, because
it tells her she can go home, up
the muddy mountain road, to La Piedad,
that her sisters will be there still,
littler than she, and she can cradle
Angelita, new and small, and sing
to her until she sleeps. But always
the song ends, in a cardboard box
draped in plastic, in the city where
the eagle talons the snake and
you have to steal to live.
                                        Oh but
angel, heavier than a man can lift,
help this woman who sinks
to the bench, so sad and dark.
Show her how even in the deepest
temblor, something will be saved.

A shaft of shine angles from the clouds,
polishing the angel's parts: robe, hands,
hair, and still intact, the wings.
                                        Teresa gets up,
passes through the museum gate out
into the street. The bougainvilla are
all in pink. It is such a pretty day,
and, though she is the oldest, Teresa
almost skips. She is so happy just
holding Angelita's hand.

Juan of the Angels

Sits in the dark bar. The hotel
no longer pays him for the songs
his fingers make on the instrument
which is the marriage of his hands.
Instead they bring him coca or cidral.
And when the bar's shadow spills
outside and the stars come out,
they bring him beer.
                                        Every day Juan
leans more deeply on his cane, but
still he comes. Guests buy him drinks.
Sometimes they stop talking. Juan
plays on, talk or none. All his
melodies are hungers.
                                        One evening
a boy, perhaps fourteen, comes in.
The boy says nothing, listens with
his eyes. Juan cradles his guitar.
Soy gitano, he says. Gypsy.
The boy, who speaks no Spanish,
thinks Juan is saying his name,
so he says *Django* and points to
his own thin chest. Juan offers
him the guitar, with its mouth
of mother of pearl, and the small
moons along the frets.
                                        The boy
bends over. His dark hair falls
across his face. He makes the song

young Juan would play for the women
to dance. All night, the same strum.
The women's skirts whirl around
the long fires. The stars are
turning pale.
The boy plays on alone.

Waiting for the Bus

She casts the only shade at the crossroads.
She has set the huge basket down
full of sticks to sell,
which she slings with her rebozo over
her shoulder.
                    Her bare feet feel the dust
no more than stones do, but there is beginning
in her head
               a sort of flying.
                                   She counts
the ribs of a cow, shifting under its stretched
skin as it mouths the sparse grass between
the rocks.
               She sings to herself, a song with
her name:
        Si Adelita se fuera con otro, la seguiría
por tierra y por mar
                         but the heat is a dry sea
and a wind is coming up and she is feeling
what she felt when she first saw the young
soldier in his glorious uniform, her Juan
who died this morning,
                         his few coins arranged
in the dirt by the bruja to stop the pain,
the bruja who took the coins and went away.
And somehow

Adela's smooth braids are turning
to wings, and the road is spinning, and *Ay*
she thinks, soaring above the desert, free
in the hard blue sky.
He is seeking me by air.

The Liberator

She is five years old, wearing pink ruffles and shiny black shoes, and socks white as candles. Mamá is taking her to see the murals. Mamá tells her how Hidalgo's army set fire to the Alhondiga, how they burst in and killed everyone inside. Even the women, Mamá says. She tells her how, since Hidalgo was a priest and his cause was just, the Virgin of Guadalupe watched over him that day. It was a great victory, Mama says. For freedom. They are walking into a patio. She looks up and sees Hidalgo there, painted huge across the arches. The padre's hands are open. But it is his eyes that catch the orange flames around him, his eyes that cover her body with burns.

She is twenty. She wears jeans to class. She leaves nervous red rings on her cigarettes. She has learned to dance, pressed to the small movements of Guillermo's hips. Yet sometimes the cross on Mama's bedroom wall seems to glow, and she feels an edge to her fingers as though they do not know quite what to do. And some nights the clothes on her chair seem to take shape. And rise. And they are taller than all her dreams and the shadow they cast is tinged with orange, like the light under the door of a burning room. And sometimes she thinks her own life, her breasts, her legs, her deep black hair, is a prison, and that she will never escape.

La Senora de Garcia-Marcos Considers

Can I cover me with a snake?
Shall I span my mouth with colored wings?
How I have wished for a wooden face
that will not melt!

His slaps will leave no marks on me.
If his kisses wear me thin, I can
paint me back. I will show a smile
as beautiful as a rock. I will

wear the hat of some high office.
If I enter a room, gasps will follow.
I will talk freely then, flashing
my jeweled wrists and hands.

4

Uchepas

Tamales plain-steamed then whitened
like a wedding dress, with cream
and queso. A beautiful, simple food.
And not enough. We want more.

We are cravers of storms and choques
on the highway. We never mind
waiting in the long stopped lines
if at the end there can be some blood.

Forget our lovers. We want a stranger,
shiver deepest at the hairs on the
backs of someone's hands, who
has not touched us, yet.

Guayabas

Puckered pears
arranged in hard pyramids on the stone.
Beneath green rind, white flesh.
The curve of the guayaba,
the curve of my palm.

An Indian woman,
not young, heavy in her striped skirt.
Her long braids, deeper than starlings'
wings. In the slowly falling light
the curve of her cheek.

The Meaning of Taquitos

She flips bits of meat into small limp
tortillas, arranges them in petals on
a heavy green plate, splashed with swans.
I choose one, drown it in salsa. When she
looks away, I look down, into the pot
at the simmering head, its horns gone
its eyes out its flesh shredded. Only
the jawbone does not yield, the jaw
with its flat teeth sunken in, like
an instrument a squatting man might
play

He grips the jaw between his knees,
drums with bones sheened opium by
the moon And his voice is a low bowl
and his hands...his hands are
quickening

How long has this indio
been standing beside me, salsa dripping
between his fingers, his mouth rimmed
red? A few moments. Thousands of years.

In The Market, Jesús Cleans Fish

One slick hand slides in,
comes up jeweled. Red ropes,
slithers of veiny pink.
fall to his brimming tub.

The other holds the fish.
So silver is this fish.
The air inside it breathes
like Lupe sleeping. He

strokes its slippery flesh,
rolls it between his fingers.
No. Not like Lupe sleeping.
Like Lupe when she moans.

Dog

The dog on the roof leans snarling.
His ribs grin from his side.
His lips peel back like fruit.
His gums are pale blood, and wet.

The street is littered with mango
skins and feces.   Dirty water
runs along the stone. The stucco
is falling from the houses.

The dog on the roof leans snarling.
The hairs rise on my arms.
I want the dog.

Casa

I am walled and atop my walls
are glass teeth.
Sharp jewels of green and amber.
Clear shards to catch the light
the way a bride turns her ring.

Inside, soft red flowers open.
Inside, yellow bougainvilla glitters
like the yellow specks in my eyes.
Oh if you would be a thief
come crawling. Come bleeding.
Come to me in ribbons.

Blood

In the market a bull's skinned head.
Horned still, with black lips.
A boy is carving from the cheek,
slides the slices off his palm.
Green flies gather on the cuts
like jewels.
            In the disco-bar
Amalia, inside her thin black
dress. Rafael, who is gone,
used to hurt her. A perfume
drifts from Amalia's skin.
Men buzz, oil their hair,
hurry across the room.

El Grito de Dolores

A bus passes.
I drink its sweet black air.
The bus jumped the curb, cornering.
The bus slammed through the potholes.
I want to do that too.
With my rear-view mirror hung with saints.
With my radio blaring *Guadalajara.*
As if it were always night and I drunk
banging through the unlit streets
past the bars with their half-doors
past the tequila factory
past Tlaquepaque   rattling fast
in the wrong lane.   You Martín
with your macho fists. You with your
wet lips.   Get off the road.

Chiles: A Birthday Poem

Lanterns, orange and veined
Hot red birds
Green fires

Long dry withered maroons
with seeds that rattle
like old men full of passion...

You in the front row, whispering
to your companion wearing pearls,
I no longer care what you think
I will be who I am

Final

Me moriré en Paris con aguacero.
-Vallejo

I will die in Tonalá among the ceramic hamburgers.
I think I will have in my hand some very small
souvenirs- a duck, a doll's olla, a tiny snake.
And these will be like what I have tried to make
with grains of words fired hard. Something for
your child. And the duck will not have real wings,
but painted ones, done by the eyelashes
of dreams. And the olla will hold a comida
whose sweetness you can hardly imagine because
you cannot smell so small. And the snake
will be a good snake. When I am gone, it can
curl in your heart.
And it will be the weather
of my abuela, whose hair brooked no white,
her Mexico, of hard skies blue as the rim
of a glass. And I will not fall. I will simply
sit down, by a little girl in ragged pink
and her friend with the dusty knees, who
are playing a game among some boxes because
at that moment, more than I have ever wanted
anything in my life, I will want to play too.

Glossary and Notes

abuela: grandmother

agua caliente: literally "hot water", here refers to a hot spring, which is gushing high into the air

arepas: a typical food of central Mexico, made from a base of masa harina (corn flour) with various fillings

barrato: cheap

bobo: clown

bruja: witch

buñuelos: sweet rolls

caballo: horse

camión: city bus

canciones: songs

cerveza: beer

choques: accidents (car wrecks)

coca and cidral: coca cola, and an an apple-flavored soft drink

conjunto: a musical group

cuando morimos: when we die

Django: Django Reinhart was a famous French jazz guitarist.

El Grito de Dolores: the rallying cry for the Mexican war of independence from Spain in the early 19th century. Dolor means pain. Lola is a nickname for Dolores.

espéranos: wait for us

dulces: sweets

estrella: star

Guadalajara: a rousing song from the state of Jalisco, of which Guadalajara is the capital

guayaba: a green fruit

ja ja: ha ha (joke)

la Virgen: the virgin, ie Mary

Los Viejitos: literally "little old men"; a dance from Michoacan made up by indians, to mock the Spanish

maguey: the cactus plant from which tequila is made

mariachi: a band which plays traditional music, especially of Jalisco state

masa: the dough of masa harina, a kind of corn flour from which tortillas are made

mercado: market

milagro: miracle

nombres: names

nopales: the fleshy leaves of cactus, sold sliced

olla: a clay cooking pot

pájaros: birds

Palacio del Gobierno: city hall

para las moscas: for the flies

peluquero: barber

platanillo: a large red iris-like flower which grows in damp places

PRD and *PRI* are political parties.

presidente municipal: mayor

queso: cheese

rebozo: shawl

Si Adelita se fuera con otro, la seguiría por tierra y por mar: a line from a traditional folk song where a young man sings of his love; translation "if Adelita should leave with another, I'd follow her by land and sea"

sierra: mountain range (and also the name of a fish caught in Pátzcuaro's lake)

Sobre Transportes del Norte: About "Transportes del Norte", literally Northern Transport, a bus line

temblor: earthquake

the eagle talons the snake: In legend, the founders of Mexico City were shown where to build by an eagle with a snake in its claws which alit there.

Three Stars of Gold: Tres Estrellas de Oro is a Mexican bus company.

uchepas: breakfast tamales typical of Michoacan

Yo soy de: I'm from (Salinas)